MIKE TANNER

A HIGHLY SUCCESSFUL PARTNERSHIP

SUCCESS AND HAPPINESS - WHAT YOU
ACHIEVE IN LIFE IS UP TO YOU

MIKE TANNER

A HIGHLY
SUCCESSFUL
PARTNERSHIP

SUCCESS AND HAPPINESS - WHAT YOU
ACHIEVE IN LIFE IS UP TO YOU

MEREO
Cirencester

Mereo Books

1A The Wool Market Dyer Street Cirencester Gloucestershire GL7 2PR
An imprint of Memoirs Publishing www.mereobooks.com

A highly successful partnership: 978-1-86151-223-9

Cover design - Ray Lipscombe

The address for Memoirs Publishing Group Limited can be found at
www.memoirspublishing.com

The Memoirs Publishing Group Ltd Reg. No. 7834348

The Memoirs Publishing Group supports both The Forest Stewardship Council® (FSC®)
and the PEFC® leading international forest-certification organisations. Our books carrying
both the FSC label and the PEFC® and are printed on FSC®-certified paper. FSC® is the
only forest-certification scheme supported by the leading environmental organisations
including Greenpeace. Our paper procurement policy can be found at
www.memoirspublishing.com/environment

Typeset in 11.5/17pt Plantin
by Wiltshire Associates Publisher Services Ltd.
Printed and bound in Great Britain by Printondemand-Worldwide, Peterborough PE2 6XD

CONTENTS

I dedicate this book with love to my wife Barbara.

FOREWORD

I was inspired to write this account of my life by my concern at the ever-increasing pessimism promoted now by all areas of the media, which seems to be targeted towards destroying all hope for future generations. It must be very depressing for the young to be bombarded constantly by this talk of gloom, from global warming and climate change to corruption in banking, business and politics and the abject failure of the education system to equip youngsters for a productive life.

My answer to this is to be optimistic and proactive. Don't listen to Twitter and your so-called friends - make up your own mind. To help with this I present the following somewhat, but not exclusively, autobiographical record, for I occasionally go off on a complete tangent.

It should be remembered that in the 1930s to 1960s, you were expected to fail in life if you did not pass the eleven-plus and go to grammar school. Not true, as I hope this record will show. In the same way it is now being said that you must go to university to get a good job and be successful; again, not true.

In this respect, relative to my failure and my brother's success at the eleven-plus examination, I have been able to illustrate pass and fail results and draw a possible conclusion in the final chapter of these memoirs.

I have introduced a thread of social comment throughout, in order to relate to the modern era. I have also sometimes related my life experiences to world events of the time. There is no fictional element, although I may have excluded some experiences which I have no desire or need to recall.

To identify people, I have sometimes used nicknames and forenames, but they are the original ones; otherwise the whole history would not seem real to me. In the same way, because I have traced my work experiences and progress through to senior management, I have had to explain in some detail, without going into the specific technologies, how the promotions and transitions came about.

CHAPTER 1

1933 – A YEAR TO REMEMBER

Many people may not fully appreciate the significance of 1933, but this was the year when England's Harold Larwood blitzed the Australians in the Ashes with his bodyline bowling, and even Don Bradman was unable to halt the England success.

It was also the year when Adolf Hitler became the German Chancellor. Now I doubt if the Führer had ever heard of Larwood, for the 'play up and play the game' spirit of cricket was hardly a Germanic principle in those now far-off days. He had a much more serious blitzing principle up his sleeve.

Also Herr Hitler, as far as I knew at the time, was completely unaware of a far more significant event, for I was born in Coventry in September of that year. I did however wonder later, when I was about seven, if he had actually been aware of this when he, in a very non-cricket way, blitzed Coventry in 1940, killing 585 people and injuring a further 1600, whilst completely destroying the centre of the city in one night. But if he did know about me, his spy network had obviously failed him, for I had moved to South Birmingham some time in 1934.

Of course the real reason for the family move to Birmingham during the very deprived early thirties was economic, following the 1929 Wall Street banking crash. Unemployment was far worse than the situation following the 2009 banking failure. The difference was the complete lack of any helpful benefit system. If you were out of work, your family was in abject poverty. My father would never allow this and always made sure he had a job, but this of course meant you had to move wherever necessary. This procedure, now described sometimes as part of 'social mobility', seems to be unacceptable in these modern times. The principle of 'getting on your bike' referred to by the ex-chairman of a political party was roundly condemned by the media.

To expand on this mobility principle, my father, Charles George Tanner, was a Cockney, born and bred in 1906 in Bow, a district of Poplar in London, but because of his eventual grammar school education (I shall refer to this later), he lacked any noticeable accent, even though he could, in later years, much to the amusement of myself, younger brother and sister relapse into the vernacular slang of 'apples and pears' etc . There was never any bad language allowed in the family home, even to the extent that your bottom, if it had to be smacked because you were naughty, was your 'BTM'. Seems silly to most people, now that we are subjected to the constant and completely unnecessary foul language even very young children hear from television on a daily basis. In this respect I find it nauseating to hear the ridiculous screaming applause for foul-mouthed so-called comedians in many television shows. I immediately use the 'off' button. Whatever happened to the principle taught even when I was at school, that the constant use of the vernacular just demonstrates that you have a poor vocabulary?

Is it true that RADA have moved from the Method school of acting, which in itself makes it very difficult to follow the plot in productions, due to the mumbling diction, to a principle of developing many innovative ways of expressing sexual swearwords, to make it sound more interesting, even though you do not understand what it's all about?

Anyway, to return to the theme of social mobility, my father left home at the age of fourteen before completing his education, due I guess to some family break up, although I was never told about this. Suffice it to say that my paternal grandfather was described as 'deceased' on my parents' marriage certificate in 1932, even though I know he visited us in Birmingham in about 1939 and took us out for a ride in his car. When he did eventually die in 1958, he left a very small inheritance to my father, so all problems were presumably solved by then.

So what happened to the errant 14-year-old Charles in 1920? Suffice it to say that by the time he met his 18-year-old future wife, Ena Florence Arnold, in 1929 he had become a sales manager for the Erinmore Tobacco Co and had, very unusually in those days, a company car, a very impressive Morris Cowley. How he achieved all this in those very difficult times I will never know, but it certainly prepared him for what was to come.

The history is far from complete, but I presume that following the loss of the sales management situation, a move to and from his next job with the Alvis Motor Company and the associated temporary accommodation with a family in Coventry, became essential. This was partly necessitated by my arrival. First he obtained employment with a well-established Birmingham scientific instrument manufacturers and pharmaceutical company, Phillip Harris Ltd. Then he secured more suitable accommodation, a mid-terrace two-bedroomed council house in Riversdale Road, Birmingham, which was to be home until 1937. One of my few memories from this period is of a windmill which was visible from the back bedroom window.

Although of course I cannot remember living in Coventry, my earliest memory is actually returning for a social visit with Mother, Father and my baby brother Anthony. He must have been about 18 months old, for I can still picture him playing soap bubbles outside on the wide pavement, with the white clay pipe in his mouth (none of your plastic rubbish, this was 1937). The grown-ups were obviously reminiscing inside the house.

During the initial settling-down period, life could not have been easy at a time of deep economic depression, and of course Mother stayed at home to look after us children. She, I know, made our own and many of our relatives' clothes, using a pedal-operated Singer sewing machine. All the furniture was either second-hand or made by my father, who, I learned much later, was very keen on carpentry and indeed produced some excellent items, which remained much admired and in use for decades.

Leather shoes were repaired. I still have the three-legged shoe last used by my father in my shed. Socks with holes were darned, as absolutely nothing could be wasted.

We moved at the end of 1937 to a much more desirable three-bedroomed house with side entrance owned by a private housing association in a tree-lined road, which became available for rent. My dad was now well established in his position and in fact remained as Transport Manager with the same company until his retirement in 1971. This remained the family home, and was eventually purchased by my mum and dad, as sitting tenants, in 1950 for about £850.

The Second World War from 1939 to 1945 produced many problems.

CHAPTER 2

PRIMARY SCHOOL AND WAR

My first local primary school in 1938 was only a 10-minute walk from home. Unfortunately, after a few months, I developed a problem with my left ankle, which turned out to be a bone infection, apparently, I learned years later, probably due to TB infected cow's milk. Anyway it did mean I was away from school for an extended period, first in hospital, then at home in bed with the ankle immobilised in a plaster cast.

When the war started in 1939 I was still bedridden, but I well remember seeing the first barrage balloons going up from the vantage point of my bedroom window and my father explaining their function. I was allowed up shortly after, but needed to wear a leg-iron support for a number of years, even after I returned to school, which I think must have been towards the end of 1939.

Of course I was behind with my schooling and remained in the class below my age group, but somehow I caught up fairly quickly, not because I was clever but more probably because I had been home schooled by my mother during my time off.

My sister Prudence must have been born about this time also, but I cannot say I recall the event.

So I moved back up to my age group A stream and managed to largely ignore my leg problem and take part in all activities. This was helped considerably, when I moved into the next age grade, by the fact that the teacher, Mr Bott, was an ex-soldier who had lost a leg in the trenches in the First World War. He was an excellent teacher, if very strict, as any sign of bullying or other unacceptable behaviour resulted in the cane. I do remember him narrating the story about the message passed from the front line trenches, by mouth, starting off 'Send reinforcements we're going to advance' which when it arrived at the command post became, 'Send three and four pence, we're going to a dance'. I can almost hear him saying it even now.

One other memory remains from his class, very strange for me, I well remember singing a song:

Early one morning
Just as the sun was rising
I heard a maiden singing in the valley below
Oh don't deceive me,
Oh never leave me,
How could you use a fair maiden so?

Now I have no idea what this song was called, or why, over seventy years later, I remember this lyric and the accompanying melody. Suffice it to say that I have no recollection of any other songs sung in my school life.

Going to school during wartime was of course exciting for young boys (I'm not sure about the girls). We did not really understand or appreciate what was happening, but we were thrilled to see the occasional dogfight in the blue skies above us, as our Spitfires and Hurricanes fought the Battle of Britain with the German air invaders. We walked to school in the morning, probably after spending most of the previous night in the air raid shelter with our gas masks round our necks, searching for shrapnel from the previous night's raid. 'Mine's bigger than yours' was the ultimate brag.

This was wartime, and everything from food to clothing was subject to rationing. Your shoes, for example, very often could not be repaired, as the leather was not available. A piece of cardboard inside the shoe was the only solution.

Living on the southern outskirts of Birmingham meant that although we did have the occasional local bomb damage and houses destroyed, this was in fact only collateral damage, compared to what was happening in the central and industrial areas of this and other cities. Hundreds of thousands of people had to leave their homes for safer parts. My mother's parents, for example, had to go to live with relatives. Many thousands of others were evacuated to country locations far away.

Although I was not to know this at the time of course, my future wife Barbara lived with her parents, very close to the BSA (Birmingham Small Arms) works in Small Heath where her father worked. It was a constant night raid target for the German bombers and was eventually destroyed. This must have been horrifying in the extreme.

From then onwards, although the war still went on, junior school life was largely uneventful. My leg iron, which I was allowed to discard eventually in favour of an elastic support bandage, was mostly ignored, even though of course all the boys wore short trousers up to the age of eleven or twelve in those days.

I do recall I was never interested in poetry or drama, and the school play or concert seemed completely uninteresting to me. I did not enjoy pretending to be someone else. I was however quiet keen on other areas of learning.

Even now I recall being taught the disciplines of spelling and punctuation. I don't say I was very good at it, but the principles have stuck with me to this day.

For example, even now, I find it difficult to accept the incorrect pronunciation of the letter H - it is pronounced 'aitch', not 'haitch'. At junior school you would be laughed at by the class as being childish for a basic mistake of this type.

As another example, in class everyone was expected to read out loud extracts from books. So aged eleven, during my reading I came to the word soldier, but out came 'soljer'. 'Stop!' said the teacher. 'There is no J in soldier. Read that passage again!' So I started again and out came soljer once more, to sarcastic sniggers from all around me. What was the result, you might ask? Yes, I went about for the next few days muttering, solDiers, solDiers, solDiers, under my breath until I was almost confident I would get it correct next time.

In much later life, when helping my wife run a business, we were approached by a fairly high-profile business consultant who was to provide an accountancy package. All went well until he provided for consideration a computer disk upon which he had erroneously hand written 'proffessional package'. I looked at him and said 'No thanks, I have changed my mind, I don't wish to continue using your company'. I did not tell him it was because he sought to advise me but could not spell the word 'professional'.

School playground games, as I recall, were usually restricted to line-type competitive team games. Ball games were very rare, and any balls used were strictly controlled and not freely available, due to wartime problems. This did not suit me at all as I was becoming increasingly keen on cricket and football, unofficially discarding my ankle support of course for out-of-school activities.

In school, the eleven-plus exams loomed on the horizon. To explain the set up: the year class of about 34 pupils was arranged so that the slower learning, more disruptive children were seated closest to the teacher (I only realised this later). Those considered more able sat in the farthest row, and the top of the class at the very back. Thus the children furthest from the teacher were expected to succeed at the exam. The seating arrangement was two boys, two girls, two boys, two girls, two boys in the furthest row from the teacher.

In my case, we sat the exam at King Edward's School, Camphill. My parents and my teacher, Miss Martin, expected me to pass. I failed, but Stanley sitting next to me passed, as did, I was mortified to find, the two girls Pat and Janet sitting directly in front of me. This seemed like the end of the world to me, but my parents to their credit did not make too much of my failure.

So was I set to be a failure in life? We will find out later.

In the meantime, out-of-school activities were more exciting. At the top of our road a cinema had been built in 1937, a splendid Art Deco style building I later learned, but I was much more interested in the Saturday morning shows, with the weekly serials Wild Bill

Hickock, Deadwood Dick, The Skull and many more to look forward too. All this took second place to my football and cricket activities. On the opposite side of the road to the cinema was a small unfenced open field, known locally as Bull's Field. This was an ideal spot for our impromptu games. The local lads would put the coats down, or the stumps up, as often as possible. Of course the war was still on and there was very little organised sport; I remember for example that the convoys of American soldiers travelling along the adjacent main Alcester Road would throw chewing gum to us as they drove past.

This location was the best place to be in the area. As it was next to the cinema, we also had the opportunity to sneak in through the back door to see parts of the grown-ups' films, thanks to getting to know one of the young doormen. On reflection he must have been a bit retarded.

CHAPTER 3

A SPORTING BOYHOOD

When the war ended in 1945, there were massive street celebrations everywhere. Our party was actually held on Bull's Field, where many of the trees were cut down to fuel the bonfire. A marvellous time was enjoyed by everyone, but of course all the restrictions, including rationing and shortages of everything, continued for many years after. I remember asking my dad what would be on the news now that the war was over, and he replied, 'There are plenty of little wars going on all the time'. How right he was.

Many people in those days would have a cycle of some sort, but to a youngster it was an absolute necessity in order to keep pace with the crowd. I had a beat-up little old bike which was completely overshadowed by the smart lightweight Dawes machines of seemingly all my friends. Little did I know that this was about to change, for somehow, without my prior knowledge, my Dad hand-built a bright orange enamelled sports bike, complete with 26-inch wheels, the latest dérailleur gear change and hub brakes as a birthday present. I kept this until I was about twenty.

There was of course no television in those days, not for us anyway. I did have a crystal set in my bedroom, so with a wire dangling outside the window, I could listen in bed through my headphones to the Saturday night theatre horror stories, always read by the sinister sounding 'Man in Black'. I remember 'The Pit and the Pendulum', for example. Early in the morning before school I listened to the Ashes test matches coming all the way from Australia. The reception was surprisingly good, even if you had to scratch about with the whisker on the crystal frequently.

Bull's Field was then scheduled for development and a branch of the Birmingham Municipal Bank was built on our play area, so we had to find somewhere else to go. Fortunately the barrage balloon field in Maypole Lane, very close by, was now redundant, so we moved all our miscellaneous unofficial activities there.

I had a best friend, Philip 'Flash' Walker, twelve months older than me, who was equally sports mad. So much so that we would go to the balloon field on our own, set up single stumps and take turns batting and bowling for hours on end. He became a very good fast bowler, so I had to become a very defensive batsman, for if I missed the ball I had to run miles to retrieve it.

For fielding practice we would stand at opposite ends of the wicket and hurl the ball as hard as we could at each other - no gloves or pads. Alternatively the ball was thrown as high as possible – even then Flash had a very good arm. I remember that on one particular occasion I concentrated so hard on the plummeting ball that I ran into the three-foot deep pond.

The winter of 1946/47 was very severe, making it impossible to play football in the deep snow. In those days householders would clear the footpath outside their property, and Flash and I, being ever resourceful, would get in our individual batting and bowling practice on the cleared pavement, being super careful not to hit the hard composition cricket ball over the fence into the neighbours' front gardens.

We eventually became a little more organised in our football games, to the extent of arranging matches with other local sides and called ourselves 'Maypole Wanderers'. A local farmer, Mr Pearman, actually allowed us to mark out and play matches in among the cow pats. The erection of goal posts was a bit beyond us lads, as we were only about thirteen, so some of our parents became involved, mine included.

From this a youth club was formed, and we became members of the Birmingham Federation of Boys Clubs. Eventually after a few years, as the club grew more organised, weekly club meetings were held in the local school hall, with other activities, such as table tennis, billiards and snooker in addition to the football and cricket. Girls were eventually added to the membership, so other social events developed.

We also played table tennis matches against rival clubs, arranged through the Federation of Boys' Clubs. Now I was not very good at this sport, but I was occasionally selected, probably to make up the numbers. When it came to my turn, I saw on the score board that I was to play an 'A. Haden'. This to our surprise turned out to be an 11-year-old girl! There were no girls in our team, so I was completely deflated to lose the game without, as I recall, scoring a single point. My humiliation was only slightly reduced when it was revealed that she was the daughter of A. A. Hayden, the captain of the British table tennis team. This little girl went on, many years later, to become the Ladies' Wimbledon and Paris Lawn Tennis champion, Ann Hayden-Jones.

My mum and dad were keen ballroom dancers, hence my first involvement in the club socials - with what was to become, little did I know at the time, another interest for me in future years - but more about that later. Suffice it to say that with my parents and our next-door neighbours, I did attend dance classes at Moseley and Balsall Heath Institute for a short period. I can still remember learning, for example, the whisk, wing and open telemark, along with many other figures.

Most of my friends did not know about this closely-guarded secret activity at the time, but it did give me a certain advantage over them a few years later, when you needed to be able to dance to get the girl.

In 1946 I visited my first professional football match at St Andrews and became a lifelong supporter of Birmingham City. I can still remember all the team members' names, from Gil Merrick in goal to George Edwards on the left wing. Starting in 1947 I attended the Warwickshire School of Cricket at the Edgbaston county ground, actually in the basement below the main pavilion. All the top first team county professionals at the time were helping in this project without pay, including Warwickshire and England's Dollery and Eric Hollies, New Zealand's fast bowler Tom Prichard and the county coach, Tiger Smith. What price the modern so-called cricket academies!

We were taught very carefully all the correct techniques of batting and bowling. In this respect I still have the 1948 copy of Don Bradman's How To Play Cricket.

Health and safety came into prominence, as we were all made to wear a box protector, most of us for the first time, before facing the likes of Charlie Grove, Hollies and a half-paced Prichard.

Most cricket enthusiasts will know that in his final test for Australia at the Oval in 1948 Bradman was bowled by Eric Hollies for a duck, thus preventing him ending with a career test average of over 100. This was very significant for me, as I was able to boast to all my mates, for months afterwards (correction, I am still boasting!) that I had batted against Hollies a week previously and he did not get me out.

From the Maypole Wanderers club we also attended boxing lessons at Kyrle Hall Boxing Club. Being tall for my age and distinctly over-confident, I eventually found myself matched up with a lad three years older than me, and he absolutely murdered me. I had two black eyes and a broken nose, and I did not lay a glove on him in three rounds. I promptly gave this activity up permanently in 1948, as did Joe Louis following his victory over Jersey Joe Walcott to retain the World Heavyweight Championship in that same year.

When I look back to this time in my life, I struggle to understand how I managed to fit everything in, for I was also an active member of the Local Emmanuel Church Youth Fellowship, stewarded by the Vicar, eventually Canon Norman Power, who actually diagnosed my broken nose and was a tremendous icon for all the local youth.

I was also in the Boy Scouts, where I learned how to tie knots, earn various badges and march in the church parades. No surprise then that my school work tended to suffer somewhat, and that my gammy ankle was causing problems again. One piece of good news in that respect was that it transpired that I had not got any serious problem. The pain, stiffness and swelling were caused by synovitis, a lack of lubrication to the joint, but it was a problem likely to remain with me permanently. It has indeed done so.

CHAPTER 4

SECONDARY SCHOOL

---◦◦◦---

Following the eleven-plus failure, I went initially to an all-boys secondary modern, Wheelers Lane in Kings Heath. The emphasis there seemed to be towards areas I was not very keen on. There was too much play acting, music, singing and art. This I think was because it was not anticipated that eleven-plus failures would have the aptitude for the more academic subjects.

The predominant physical activity, gymnastics, I was not very good at, probably because of an imbalance created by my ankle. Only one activity pleased me – swimming. This involved a weekly trip to the very local Kings Heath baths. I cannot remember how I had learned to swim, but I was quite proficient, so much so that I actually taught other class members, including the form captain. Incidentally the teacher in charge never even came into the water - perhaps he couldn't swim. I count this as possibly my only enjoyable activity throughout the thankfully short time (twelve months) I spent at this school.

The Headmaster, whose nickname was Leo the Lion, was very keen on the arts, Shakespeare and choral singing. When the selection for parts in a play were taking place, I made sure I was well at the back so I did not get picked to participate. One event I remember vividly. During a singing lesson, we were aligned in rows, and the target was to sing in descant I believe. Leo came down the line listening to each boy in turn. When he got to me he said 'Boy, go and sit over there and never sing in one of my classes again'. I was not at all deflated, for I did not want to sing his silly songs anyway.

Fortunately an escape from all this dreariness was only just round the corner - the opportunity to sit the entrance examination for a commercial or technical college. I chose to go the technical route, taking the engineering rather than the building option, on advice from my dad. What a splendid decision that was.

I went along to the introduction day at Bordesley Green Technical College, and from the moment I walked up the entrance drive I knew this was for me. Halfway up the drive, on a pedestal, was a Rolls Royce Merlin engine, labelled as being from a Spitfire 609 Squadron at Biggin Hill, Battle of Britain. We were then taken on a tour round the classrooms and instruction workshops, ending with the quadrangle at the back, where an enclosed cricket practice net had been set up, with a very accomplished young batsman, who I later learnt was the school captain, displaying his skills.

The entrance examination took place a few weeks later. I remember one question from the various different papers, consisted of a rectangular box with a cross section showing an input shaft and an output result. A multitude of pivoting internal levers were shown, and the object was to highlight only those required to achieve the end action. I have always wondered if I got my answer correct to that particular question, but anyway I did pass the exam, so I was able to leave Leo to his acting and singing. He was probably also more than happy to see the back of me.

This unexpected success did however create its own problems, for at almost the same time my younger brother Tony passed his eleven plus to Kings Norton Grammar school, thus duplicating the need for expensive school uniforms. In addition, because of the specialist nature of my school, the required technical text books had to be purchased; there was no free state provision in those days.

Thus there was no alternative but to withdraw from the bank my twelve years' savings of pocket money gifts from relatives, amounting to nine pounds two shillings and sixpence. This just about covered the uniform and other costs. To show how important this was to me, I still have these books now, almost seventy years later. They are Engineering Science by Brown & Bryant (7s-6d), Mathematics for Technical Students by Geary (9s-

6d), Applied Mechanics by Morley (9s-6d) and Heat Engines by Walshaw (12s-6d).

Another problem was that the journey to and from school involved two connecting bus rides of forty minutes in total, and with the school hours being nine until five, there was no way I could continue with my paper round. This lost me my five shillings a week pocket money. The problem was resolved by my mum taking a part-time job in order to assist with the extra costs involved and the changing circumstances. This was only possible because my younger sister Prudence had conveniently now started school.

Anyway, I was settled into a good school, and following a curriculum I mainly enjoyed. My E1 class designated in the first term consisted of 34 pupils, all boys of course. The subjects were mainly science based, but there were plenty of other activities.

Despite having a 440-yard running track with a central general sporting area, once a week we went by bus to a sports ground with multiple pitches for competitive games. The same age group, building class B1, joined us. This was I think the only occasion when the two disciplines were amalgamated. We certainly considered the builders to be inferior, and they probably thought the same about us.

Even lunchtimes at Bordesley Green were exciting, and most days we would go to the British Restaurant further along Washford Heath Road. A good meal cost a shilling. Afterwards we would play a football match against the apprentices from the close by Morris Commercial Factory, on the ash-covered empty car park.

On other days we might go to the local café and waste our shilling lunch money on the electric gaming machines. I never seemed to get the highest score, and a bottle of dandelion and burdock compensated for that. Oh what a life!

The sports master, Mr Lunn, also taught science subjects. Behind his classroom desk there hung a picture of him training on Blackpool beach with England star Stanley Matthews. We were very impressed with this at first, but later we found that he was a rather surly and unhelpful individual. He was probably the only teacher I did not like at that school and he, I am sure, was the reason I later had no desire to be selected for school teams, preferring to concentrate on my out-of-school sporting activities.

All the lessons were interesting, but the one snag was that we were given homework projects nearly every day, and my over-busy life outside school very often did not leave enough time for them. For this reason my position in class gradually declined from fairly high up in the first term to distinctly middling as time went by.

Each six-month term ended with exams in all subjects. Your progress during the term was judged purely on results. In the final year E6 class of 1948, you were also required to write a 30-page thesis on a subject of choice. I selected 'water power' and spent weeks researching the subject. You could perhaps say that the final result was largely plagiarised - in a similar way, present-day university students will access the internet - but I was suitably proud of it. I kept the result for many years and can't recall what actually happened to it. I certainly did not knowingly dispose of it; perhaps it lies in the loft of one of my previous residences. If you happen to find it, please send it to me!

There was no qualification on leaving, except exemption from the first year of the National Certificate in Mechanical Engineering.

CHAPTER 5

THE APPRENTICE

During the final term at Bordesley Green we were taken on various works visits to help decide what sort of career we might like to follow. I was distinctly unimpressed with some areas of heavy engineering; drop forging, for example, I concluded was not for me. Then by an outstanding coincidence, a previous pupil at the college, who was now a toolroom manager in a very well-known company, Jarret Rainsford & Laughton Ltd, which had been bombed out of the centre of Birmingham during the Blitz, made an enquiry for a toolroom apprentice. Even more of a coincidence, the new factory was only ten minutes' walk from my home, in fact only a stone's throw from my original primary school. It was built on another piece of waste land on which I had played many a football match.

So I went for interview. The situation available was a five-year indentured apprenticeship as a plastic mould toolmaker, which would include design and drawing office training. This would also require also one day and three nights' attendance per week at technical college, studying for a National Certificate in Mechanical Engineering. I was very keen after touring the factory, where most aspects were explained to me. Plastics were the new thing at the time, so it was an ideal opportunity to get in on the ground floor. My parents agreed, as did my maternal grandfather, who was a skilled toolmaker in the motor supply industry himself and knew the company well.

I actually discovered later that this company had been the very first to become involved in plastic injection moulding in England in 1937, but it was also very diverse, having been in existence since 1860. In 1948 it employed over one thousand people with a very wide product range, including, in addition to my targeted field, short wave radio, ladies' hair accessories and much more.

A few weeks later, along I went with my father to sign the deeds of apprenticeship. The scale of pay laid out for the five-year period was of course very low; in fact it was only £1 5s per week, increasing to £1 10s after the initial three-month trial, with subsequent small annual increases up to £4 10s per week in the fifth year. The initial arrangement was that I would give my mother the £1 and I would keep the five shillings, rising to ten shillings after the successful completion of the three-month trial. Boy, would I feel rich with ten shillings a week, even though it would only be 50p in today's money!

And so my working life began. In January 1949 I turned up on the first morning and reported to the commissionaire as instructed. I was issued with clock number 880 and a clock card, so now I was just a number. I had never been just a number before, except on the football field. It was explained that I must clock in and out also at lunchtimes and should I be three minutes late, I would be docked fifteen minutes' time and my foreman would be informed. Formalities over, I was collected by the toolroom manager and introduced to the shop foreman.

I cannot remember too much about the early days, but suffice it to say that the toolmakers, about eighteen in total, were very friendly and helpful. I do recall that by convention, toolmakers, as the royalty of shop floor engineers, wore a cow gown type overall, but I had turned up at first with a boiler suit type, evidently, I found out, a distinct no no. This was soon put right in my second week.

Approximately 400 people were actually employed on this site at the time. I realised during my first few days that there was a diverse conglomeration of many functions, with which I would become familiar in due course.

Of course the first duty of the new apprentice was to make the morning tea, which was very important, especially as most of the men were travelling some distance to get to work. The management insisted that this should be completed before 8 am, and I fell down on numerous occasions as I was very often struggling to beat the three-minute clocking in deadline. The other extremely important duties were to clean down the machinery and sweep the shop floor.

My time at Bordesley Green had given me a very basic knowledge of most engineering hand and machining processes, but now I was to learn how to apply these in practice. It would not be appropriate here to go into too much specific detail, suffice it to say that toolmakers will generally be skilled in all aspects but will tend to specialise in a particular sphere. Thus during the early part of my training I would be taken under the wing of various specialists in turn. Some may describe this as a 'sitting next to Nellie' process, but you do learn, especially if this is under the ever-watchful eye of the foreman and/or manager. In conjunction with all this, attendance at technical college one day and three evenings per week began in September 1949.

One particular experience was very valuable. Most people smoked at that time. One toolmaker, Bob Wilson, who was a fitness fanatic, but also a smoker, took me on one side, sat me down, gave me a Woodbine and told me to smoke and inhale. After this I was very unpleasantly ill for about two hours. I have never smoked since.

The mould-making tool room had many diverse additional functions, including the design, manufacture and repair of jigs and fixtures for use in the production and packaging areas. The apprentices were always very much involved in these functions, as an important part of training and also to reduce the involvement of fully-skilled specialist mould makers. Thus came my first involvement with the production environment and the staff involved, who were mostly women and girls. But this certainly helped, particularly later in my career, in my appreciation of the general manufacturing processes.

Much of the area surrounding the factory was still waste land, where we were able to play impromptu football and cricket games during lunchtimes. Eventually we decided to form a cricket team and approached the company to see if they would be interested in helping. We were very pleasantly surprised to find that the family directors were very keen to support this, and also to discover that the company had actually sponsored the Birmingham Ice Hockey team and were keen on the development of company social activities.

As I was now fully involved with workplace activity and study, my involvement with the youth club ended.

So the cricket team J R & L was set up with a formal

committee, including one family director as Chairman and myself, thanks to my youth club experience, as secretary. Initially funding help came from the company, with membership fees and a legal scratch card scheme to provide continuing income.

We joined the Birmingham Parks Association Cricket League and played our home matches on Kings Heath Park. After a number of successful years we became Division One Champions. I still have the Sports Argus team photograph, but I don't look at it very often, because it only serves as a reminder that everyone is dead except me.

To continue on the cricket team theme, some years later the Company provided, as part of the now fully developed manufacturing site, a private cricket pitch. For this reason we withdrew from the parks leagues and played Midland club cricket.

During the winter the football team stuttered along without high profile management involvement. I was only involved as the team goalkeeper until my old ankle problems temporarily got the better of me and I confined my football to Saturday afternoon, watching Birmingham City.

CHAPTER 6

A PARTNERSHIP FOR LIFE

Life however was not all football, cricket, study and work, for the fairer sex now came into play, thanks to the previously-mentioned ballroom dance lessons and attending youth club social functions, together with dances at the local church hall. There were also functions at Kings Heath Baths, where the pool was emptied in the winter and a dance floor added for a regular Saturday night dance. I had plenty of opportunity to meet girls. Certainly, I had dilly-dallied with a few and therefore was not a complete novice at seventeen. We lads of course, despite the complete lack of relevant school biology lessons, knew all about the facts of life, or so we thought. The only problem was, the girls' mothers had told them not to do it and no decent girl would, not the ones I met anyway.

So I had no regular girlfriend, but this was about to change as I was soon to meet the girl I would, fall in love with, marry and live with forever.

Although there were possibly hundreds of girls working in the factory and offices, for some reason they did not seem to be of interest to me. I had my own circle of friends, and probably I was of no interest to them either. Despite this, one day an assistant in one of the production departments - his name was Norman - asked me if I would like to go out with a particular girl. I had no idea who she was at first, but having no girlfriend or other commitments the following Friday night, I agreed to meet her at a local fairground.

This turned out to be the best decision I ever made. Not so for her though, for she chose to bring along her best friend, a slim, very attractive girl in a blue mac. I was immediately smitten with her. I discovered her name was Barbara, but she did not seem interested in me, although we did go on one or two of the fairground rides together, including, I recall, the spectacular dive bomber.

I eventually managed to make a date to see her the following Sunday. What happened to the original girl I was supposed to be with during that first Friday evening I cannot remember, obviously very bad manners at the least on my part.

Where did we go on that first date? Yes, you might have guessed, I took her to a cricket match. It was at the City Transport Stadium, where a charity match involving my boyhood hero Gil Merrick and his Birmingham City football team was taking place.

Very strangely for me, I cannot remember anything about that game itself, only sitting with Barbara in among small scattered groups of other spectators on the surrounding grass. She did not tell me at the time, but it was actually her sixteenth birthday. What a way to spend your birthday, being bored at a cricket match! I did find out that she was working at the Wesleyan & General Insurance Society in Birmingham, as a trainee shorthand typist.

We started dating on regular basis, usually going to the local cinemas, of which there were three, and various local social dances. Life became very full, especially when evening classes recommenced in September.

At work I was spending my delegated time in the drawing and design office. During my time there a change was being made from the old blueprint method of copying drawings to photocopying. By an odd coincidence Barbara, who had now moved from shorthand typing to training in the accounts department, had left her job at the Wesleyan & General and was working for Copycat, the manufacturer of the equipment I was now involved in using.

Following my spell in the drawing office, I returned to the workshop to continue my practical training, and began to specialise in a particular area of skilled machining, which brought an unexpected opportunity.

The company, following the immediate post war years of austerity, decided to invest in new equipment, starting in my area. Thus I was invited by the Toolroom Manager to visit machine tool manufacturers with him to help evaluate equipment prior to purchase. This experience was to prove of immense value in my later career.

At about this time my brother Tony left grammar school and started work at the Radar Research Establishment in Malvern. I had half expected that he might go on to university, but very few people did in those days.

Many things that happened, even quite insignificant events, had an impact on my career and later life. A very good example of this certainly did not seem to have any beneficial value at the time. I accidentally sustained a serious cut to my right index finger, severing the guide. For a period of about three months I was unable to continue with my normal job, but as I would continue to get paid, due to my indentured staff status, I was seconded to the injection moulding production department.

My initial duty was to collate production information. Left-handed writing was not very easy, but I learned the principles surrounding the process control. Without going into too much detail here, it was very important that the injection moulding heating, cooling, interval time and pressures were consistently controlled.

I soon discovered that this was not being well done and introduced a system for achieving consistency. I was thus labelled the 'bighead from the toolroom' but production improved.

So I returned to my toolmaking duties. Following my accident I now had an assessed 20% loss of grip in my right hand, for which I received compensation of £90, to go with my gammy left ankle, both of which did restrict my cricket and football activities to a small extent but not my working or social life.

Most young people, both then and now, believe in social justice, fairness and equality for all. Some consider these values to be the prerogative of left-wing socialist movements, but of course they are more purely 'the centre ground of a civilised democratic society'.

I myself was a member of the Amalgamated Engineering Union. My shop steward encouraged me to attend local branch meetings and suggested that I should make a claim against the company relative to my injury, but as this was a complete accident and no one was to blame except myself, I was not inclined to do this.

However attendance at these meetings, which were largely populated by semi-skilled and unskilled workers in the motor and allied trades, did reinforce my common-sense view that the trade unions very militant anti-business activities at the time were taking us in the wrong direction. The constant strikes and work-to-rule restrictions throughout many industries, without in most cases any justification, were led by Red Robbo and similar communist-backed, extremely militant leaders, who were trying to lead the organised labour movement towards totalitarian Soviet principles. This resulted in disillusionment with the trade union movement, particularly by skilled and responsible workers, myself included. I cancelled my membership and decided I would fight my own battles.

Very importantly these communist principles were eventually rejected, even by the Russian people many years later, but unfortunately not before most of British manufacturing industry had been destroyed by union militancy. Margaret Thatcher came along three decades too late to prevent this demise.

Putting all these extraneous political distractions to one side, I was getting near the end of my apprenticeship in 1953 when Barbara and I became engaged. I was still only earning £4 per week compared to Barbara's £6, but between us we started to save to get married.

On completion of my indentured period, I was due for National Service. My service number was SGT 37473, and the time came for the medical. To our relief, my gammy left ankle and my faulty right index finger, combined with the discovery that I was partially colour blind (I still dispute this), conspired to make me medically unfit for duty.

Although I make light of my ankle, it has remained a considerable restriction to my activities almost throughout life. I could not walk over rough ground without suffering agonising pain and stiffness during the walk and afterwards. If I sat for any length of time I had a very painful limp afterwards, which could only be reduced by forcing the joint to move. Obviously in normal life I could plan around these problems, but this would not be possible in a military environment. They were quite correct to reject me, but Barbara didn't do so, I am glad to say.

So I was free. No more technical college with its vector diagrams, differential calculus, steam tables and night classes, but more importantly I now had the facility to move onto a fully skilled rate of pay. I would actually be earning more than Barbara, and we would be able to save properly for our wedding. I had established myself by now on a most advanced piece of equipment and was thus able to negotiate a top pay rate.

On June 4th 1955 Barbara and I married at the Emanuel Church, Highters Heath. Brother Tony, now doing National Service and studying electronics, was my best man. Everything went well. The reception was held at the Co-Op Hall in Maypole Lane, not far from that old Barrage Balloon Field with its childhood memories.

The honeymoon was not to be the elaborate affair of today. Virtually no one had cars and flying abroad was a business activity only, as the package holiday hadn't been invented. We were to go to Bigbury-on-Sea, North Devon, in a caravan. Disaster struck the day before, when a rail strike was called. Panic stations! How do we get there now?

We managed to find a taxi service willing to take us down to Devon throughout the night, though it took about eight hours. The specially-negotiated cost was £14, a big hole in our budget but unavoidable. The driver brought along his little boy, aged about eight years, who had never seen the sea. On arrival at about 6 am, we made them a cup of tea but we had no milk. What a way to spend your wedding night!

Although Bigbury was only a very quiet fishing village, it was and still is well known because of the low tide tractor sea crossing to the Burgh Island Art Deco Hotel of Agatha Christie Fame, which of course we visited, returning a number of times over the following years. It still remains now, almost exactly as it was in 1955. The rail strike continued, but we were able to arrange return by coach back to Birmingham a week later.

Initially we were to live with Barbara's parents, who had very kindly given up their large main bedroom and moved into her old room. There was no water supply upstairs, but we did make this largest bedroom into a flat, with wash stand and Baby Belling cooker. We were very determined that this was only to be a short-term arrangement while we saved for our own house. Very few of our friends had their own houses, so we lived very economically for the next two years in order to achieve this goal. I had what was now a secure well paid job and Barbara was also well paid, as a bookkeeper secretary for a shopfitting business, taking the accounts to trial balance prior to the professional accountants' involvement. I must admit that, at the time, I myself had very little understanding of debits, credits and the double-entry bookkeeping principles she was working with, but the potential for a satisfactory building society mortgage application was therefore now in place.

The criteria for a successful application were very strict and closely controlled. The maximum mortgage was no more than 3.5 times the husband's confirmed annual earnings, or alternatively 2.5 times that plus the wife's confirmed annual earnings. The earnings details would always be confirmed with the employer, so you could not cheat and obtain a mortgage greater than any lender considered viable.

Maximum mortgage advance was also restricted to 90% of Building Society valuation, which was, almost invariably, less than the buying price. How very different it was then to the lack of control which went a long way towards causing the 2008 sub-prime lending financial crisis.

So in 1956 the parameters were in place for us to

explore the options for a new home of our own. A new build of six semi-detached houses became available in Brook Lane, Kings Heath, and we approached the agent, selected our desired plot and visited the Borough Building Society to arrange a mortgage. Following a very in depth interview with the manager, a 90% 25-year repayment mortgage advance was approved, subject to a property valuation and checks with my employer of course. The purchase price was £2000, so the deposit would be £200. What we did not realise at this time was that the building society valuation would be only 80% of the purchase price. The balance to the mortgage advance would need to be through a mortgage guarantee insurance policy. This was an unexpected blow to our budget plans, but of course we went ahead. The advance was made through stage payments during the building time, and eventually in 1957 our dream of home ownership became reality.

Today, after 57 years of home ownership, I still believe that this mortgage insurance scheme was some sort of a scam, perhaps similar to the current time payment protection insurance fiasco.

Anyway, we soon settled in. Furnishing a complete house was a problem at first, but both our families helped and Barbara's earnings were of significant importance. There were no trips down to DFS, with four years to pay, as is the modern practice.

The garden was a problem, as it had been left like a rubbish heap by the builders. I was never very keen on gardening, but Barbara's dad did a tremendous job, coming up to sort it out.

I should mention that shortly after our marriage, I was best man to my friend Bob Timms on his marriage to Joan. Bob was a close colleague at work throughout my apprenticeship and afterwards. By a very strange coincidence Bob had spent his early life in Daimler Road, only just round the corner from the Riversdale Road house where I had lived until the age of four, though I cannot remember if I knew him then.

The following year the four of us went on a caravan holiday together, visiting Bigbury and the adjacent Burgh Island Hotel. Shortly afterwards Bob left the company to work for a very high-paying contract toolmaking business in Tile Hill, Coventry. Highly skilled plastic mould toolmakers were a rare breed and very much in demand.

I had now also secured a position with a different company, but much closer to hand in South Birmingham. However when I gave notice, I was called for by the Managing Director, no less. This was completely unexpected. He asked my reasons for leaving, and I explained about the considerable pay differential. He said that he could not possibly match this, as it would upset all the established pay structures, but he did not want me to leave. Would I be interested in setting up and running a new special production department?

Now I knew a little about this project from my association with the machine development department designer, who was also an ex-apprentice. I had also become familiar with the specific production process itself, during my successful cut finger secondment. So as I said before, nothing happens without a reason - even a cut finger can evidently have advantages.

After a few moments' consideration, I agreed to this offer. I said 'What about the other company I was due to join?' The MD got up out of his chair. 'Use my telephone' he said. Then he went out of his office, leaving me to do the dirty deed. Well, what a momentous decision that was, for it altered my career future profoundly.

Much more importantly, on 29th December 1958 our beautiful daughter was born. We had gone to stay with Barbara's mum and dad over Christmas. At 8 am that morning I had to call the ambulance service to take Barbara to the Sorrento Nursing Home. Husbands were definitely not allowed then. I telephoned at 12.30 pm and was told rather brusquely not to bother them, as it was far too soon. I was told to ring back later in the afternoon. I rang again at 2 pm and was told we had a baby girl, born at 1.30, and everything was fine. I was a dad!

Before the birth we did not know if we would have a boy or girl. We knew that the only known detection method, dangling a needle over the pregnant tummy and watching which way it spun, was just an old wives' tale.

But we were film fans, and Barbara knew that if it was a girl she would be christened Kim Elizabeth. Of course Kim Novak and Elizabeth Taylor were arguably the two most beautiful stars in the world at the time, and Barbara's mother's name was Elizabeth.

I do not recall whether we actually discussed names if the baby had been a boy, but probably Burt (Lancaster), Fred (Astaire), Gene (Nelson) or Errol (Flynn) would have been a definite no. Perhaps Cary (Grant) Stewart (Grainger) Clarke (Gable) or Rock (Hudson) were possibles, but on reflection not Rock - especially not Rock, what a silly name.

About ten days' stay in the nursing home was the norm then, and during this time visiting was restricted to husbands only and for very short specific times. This was the middle of winter and a heavy snowstorm meant the nurses had to clear a path for visitors through the grounds. I can't imagine this happening in modern times, as health and safety regulations would undoubtedly come into play.

Anyway, the time came at last for mother and baby to come home. We had no car of course, so the journey had to be made by taxi. Because of the extreme cold, I had bought Barbara a fur coat to come home in, but unfortunately for me, I had chosen a size eighteen and Barbara was back to a size ten. It completely swamped her, but at least it was useful to cuddle Kim Elizabeth in on the way home.

So domestic life began in earnest. Kim was a very good baby, and she slept through the night almost from the start. We had no sleepless nights, as we understood were the norm in most cases.

Barbara had to give up her job some time before the birth, and there was of course no such thing as maternity leave, and anyway she was going to be a full-time mother. She had saved for and reserved a top of the range white Silver Cross pram with a pink rose on the side. I seem to remember she paid about £26 for it, which was about three weeks' wages at the time, or the equivalent of about £1200 in today's money, but it was well worth the cost. Very proud we were to take Kim Elizabeth out in it.

So there we were, Barbara with all the domestic hard slog, me swanning off every day to play with machines and things and coming home exhausted for my dinner. I hasten to add that I still had the energy to play cricket every Sunday, also to ensure that Barbara helped with tea interval refreshments. I mean, you have to get full value for your investments, don't you!

When Kim was about two, Barbara had a part-time retail Saturday job in a record shop, where all the youngsters came to listen to and buy the latest records they had heard on Top of The Pops on the previous Friday evening. She knew all the lyrics to the latest sensations and still does even now, something that was completely outside my comprehension. I was, and in fact still am to this day, firmly stuck in the swing and dance band era of Glen Miller, Jimmy and Tommy Dorsey and the rest, with the sounds of saxophone and clarinet, to blend with perhaps Bing Crosby, Nat King Cole or even Satchmo.

CHAPTER 7

THE LEARNING CURVE

As I outlined in the last chapter, I was now deeply involved in developing a new production department. Without going into specific technical details, the object was to improve process productivity and flexibility and reduce manufacturing costs. This was to be achieved partially through the introduction of specially-designed machinery made in house. Some experience of the potential for automation existed, but progress had been restricted, as there were no UK machine builders in this specialist field.

Alongside the prime technical aspects of this project I was very keen to be involved in all aspects in order to advance my career and therefore continued my studies. I went to evening classes to study works management, resulting three years later in my passing the examination qualification for membership of the Institute of Works Managers. I now had letters after my name – MIWM.

This study gave an insight into all aspects of

management, which I was able to develop alongside the practical application of my developing process knowledge. I have detailed some of the events of the learning curve, purely to demonstrate that you need to be proactive in all directions in order to progress.

The costing system was long established in this hundred-year-old family-run business, but it was suitable more for a factoring business (which it originally was) than for the manufacturing business which it had metamorphosed into. For example stock was valued at material cost only, and no element of labour and overhead was included. Thus any year on year waste of individual resources and related inefficiencies were hidden. Conversely improvements could not be highlighted. So the reasons behind any improvement or decline in overall company performance could not be identified.

Overheads were applied in a general way, being related to direct labour costs as a standard percentage, applied almost company wide, dependent on the profit and loss trading results from the previous year. For this reason it was not possible to make cost justification calculations for alternative ways of achieving results. Value engineering and value analysis could not be undertaken. The overall company budget was not broken down into the very diverse manufacturing areas.

I identified the need for a machine-hour rate costing

system and set out to establish the principles very much in my own time, for I was already fully committed to the day-to-day practical engineering problems surrounding me.

In due course I produced a report, which I presented to the Company Accountant and Managing Director. The principles were eventually accepted and adopted. This enabled me to present a more accurate cost justification for any new methods.

Relative to this, the official company auditors were now insisting that labour and overhead costs should be included in stock valuations. This slotted in very conveniently with the now more accurate overhead content being calculated. Of great importance to me, because of the more obvious cost advantages being presented by my programme of automation, my department expanded by a factor of ten and became the cornerstone of the Plastic Division's manufacturing facility.

Alongside the improved costing facility, I also introduced more effective effort-based work study and payment incentive systems.

So all was going well on the work front for me, but I was absolutely sure there was more to come, and I was ambitious for promotion.

On the home front we now had our first car, a two-tone 1951 Morris Oxford, which was mechanically reliable and looked reasonable on the outside. Fortunately this was before the MOT test was introduced, so the fact that there was considerable corrosion to the hidden parts of the bodywork, including a large hole in the floor under the driver's side carpet mat, was not thought too serious. We were mobile and able to go on a number of holidays. We kept the Morris for a few years, and I did all the maintenance including replacing brake shoes, clutch, exhaust and decoking the side-valve engine.

This car had the old fashioned semaphore type direction indicators, which frequently did not cancel on centring the steering. I well recall on one particular occasion when I was driving along being hailed by loudspeaker from a following police car which I had failed to notice: 'KVR 603, cancel your indicator!'

Regardless of its recurring problems, the old Morris did give us the opportunity for travelling, and we had a number of very enjoyable seaside caravan holidays, usually in Wales. This started a lifetime's involvement with cars. The Morris was replaced with a Ford Consul Mk 2 and so forth, and so on ad infinitum. I have lost count of how many cars there were and shudder to think of the total depreciation involved.

My first new car was a 1964 Vauxhall Viva A type, which I think may have been the worst car I have ever owned. Vauxhall were one of the first manufacturers to adopt an acrylic paint finish, as compared with the industry standard cellulose, and they made much of this in their marketing, but I had only had the car a few weeks when the paint started to peel off in two-inch diameter patches. So I had to go back and forth to have this corrected.

No sooner had this been attended to than an engine rattle developed, and again back it went for correction. On driving the vehicle home a week later, after a so-called engine rebuild, misfiring, pinking and very poor performance were evident, even though the original cylinder rattle seemed improved.

Unfortunately it was then Saturday lunch time and the main agent's garage was closed for the weekend. I decided to investigate, only to find that the distributor setting was too far advanced. I marked the flange so that I could return it to its starting position, and because I did not have the required strobe equipment, I adjusted it by trial and error in order to achieve even running.

The following Monday morning I was round at the garage to complain in the strongest possible way, stopping just short of actually blowing my top. They of course tried to argue, but they were eventually convinced, although only after resetting and testing. The faulty distributor was then replaced.

Being more than disappointed so far with the service performance, I decided to ask the service mechanic concerned (these days they are called service technicians) a basic question which I knew a mechanic from any independent garage would be able to answer with ease. It was, 'What is the series of events in a four stroke internal combustion petrol engine?' I was not at all surprised when he did not have not a clue what I was talking about. The answer of course is induction, compression, ignition, exhaust.

So even way back in 1964, vehicle main agent service people did not have the knowledge or skills to actually diagnose or repair faults, only to change parts.

CHAPTER 8

THE GREEN GREEN GRASS OF ROAM

Before Kim started school in 1963, we decided to move to a detached house in Hollywood - not the one in the USA but in Worcestershire, about four miles away but quite close to both our parents' houses. I was still playing cricket, with Barbara's teatime cucumber-sandwich pavilion input for the home matches. I had also taken on part-time groundsman duties, so I could only blame myself if a perfect batsman's wicket did not result.

My football activities had declined, for they were causing too many ankle problems after each game. Even though I was getting the centre half to take my goal kicks, I had a painful limp for days afterwards. In any event the team did fold at this time.

In the meantime at work, the principle of building our own production equipment, born out of necessity many years earlier, was being overtaken by technological developments driven by the research of large international groups. It was no longer viable to continue building our own equipment. Suitable equipment had to be sourced instead. We had a subsidiary company in Australia which, without our internal machine building facility, had already needed to adopt this course of action. Therefore there was pressure from the group board, in the interests of consistency, to follow and purchase the same equipment. I did not agree with their choice of Australian-built machinery, having already started to search for the most technically advanced and productive equipment available. An impasse was developing.

At this time I had also undertaken some subcontract component production for a large motor industry based manufacturer. This project was very successful, so much so that I met the senior management of that company - not to put too fine a point on it, I was head hunted. After a great deal of thought, for I did not really want to leave what was a secure position of long standing, I decided to accept the position offered. Possibly the 50% salary increase may have influenced me somewhat!

I did buy my first brand new car at this time, the Vauxhall Viva, and what a load of rubbish that turned out to be, as already detailed.

So in 1965 I joined Wilmot Breeden Ltd. What a culture shock this was, compared with the paternalistic family environment I had been used to since joining from school.

To make sense of the next few years it is necessary to include a certain amount of detail. I have excluded specific reference to the detail of any technologies involved, but everything I experienced was of importance for my later career.

This company was supplying the motor and other industries with a very diverse range of manufactured products on a subcontracted basis, which was very different to producing proprietary goods for sale to the wholesale market, the business to which I was accustomed. The customers included Jaguar, Rolls Royce, Ford, Singer Sewing Machines, Hotpoint, British Motor Corporation and many more. We were manufacturing a diverse range of components such as steering wheels, door lock components, armrests, badges, door handles, salad bins and chairs.

Production control to ensure optimum use of resources was very involved, as the scheduled requirements of these customers were completely independent of each other.

The principle was supposed to be: overall total order, monthly schedule, weekly call off. Rarely did it work to plan, which created what can only be described as a complete shambles.

Within this environment it was easy to see how the

factory floor had become disorganised, with gangways almost constantly blocked and difficult to keep clean.

Giving myself time to absorb this general environment, I concentrated initially in familiarising myself with all the different manufacturing processes. I was working on the principle that if you don't fully understand the process, you cannot expect to manage it successfully.

During this time I became aware that actual output being achieved in virtually all areas was well below optimum, in some cases less than 50% of potential. How could this be? I soon found out when I put a stopwatch on one or two processes to see what the potential output was. The immediate reaction was that this was the function of the work study engineer. The values had been agreed with the Trade Union representative and were not negotiable. In many cases the processes had not been optimised prior to the negotiated values being agreed.

This was obviously a very difficult problem to overcome, for it manifested itself in many different ways. As an example, the injection moulding department ran supposedly on a continuous 24-hour basis, as is essential for optimum results for this process. Interrupted running causes high proportions of scrap and material waste. I was becoming exasperated at the overall lack of machine and material productivity, even though the production employees were easily making their incentive earnings.

On one specific occasion, I visited the plant during the night shift at 1.30 am, to find virtually no machines in production and almost all the employees fast asleep in obviously well prepared, if hidden away, bunk beds. How many years this had been going on before my arrival and involvement I did not know, but it was counterproductive to the need to improve performance and had to stop. My negotiations with the supposedly militant Trade Union to achieve this were initiated after a visit from the Main Board Managing Director. Contrary to what I had been led to expect, the Trade Union negotiator was compliant and receptive to my suggestions. The shop steward, who was also involved, was actually a tool setter in the department and understood the practical problems.

Little could be done about existing incentive values, which would remain, but the union's unofficial upper incentive ceilings, which were the cause of mid and end of shift shut downs, would be abolished. All future processes would be optimised prior to incentive levels being applied. Thus material and machine capacity use would be optimised. Overall productivity should improve.

I should point out here that if I had been able to introduce the measurement and control elements I had developed for my previous company, this would have been much more effective. I was not however prepared to bang my head against a brick wall. I decided to be satisfied with the considerable progress made, and perhaps try some further changes later.

Having resolved some serious practical problems, which produced a very noticeable improvement in performances all round, I was more than concerned to find that this was not reflected in the monthly trading results. Try harder, I thought, but no, the second month was even worse. So I invited myself into the accounts department under the pretext of exploring costing details. Money was obviously being wasted somewhere.

What I found was absolutely astonishing. During the previous twelve months' trading, large quantities of items, rejected by various customers' quality control, had been received back, but had not been debited to the divisional accounts. These returns were being applied to the current trading year whenever results hid this factor. So as performance improved, trading results did not.

I had, in fact already discovered a serious problem with internal quality control procedures, which I concluded was the cause of the previous year's returns.

The plant of necessity ran on a 24-hour shift system, but quality patrol inspection was normal days only. Thus the first quality job each morning was the belated check of the previous night's output. It was too late if there were problems. The only solution, the introduction of quality control checking on a balanced shift basis, was soon arranged, with a noticeable reduction in rejected components.

I encountered many other problems in my first year with this company, some relative to poor costing and estimating techniques, but I had considerable concerns relative to the poor maintenance condition of much of the production equipment, most of which was antiquated and inefficient, to say the least. When I made mention of this to the Works Manager, his response was 'you knew about this before you joined us'. I was appalled at this response. He did not begin to understand or appreciate how much greater productivity an investment in modern machinery would give us in this specialised area.

Very fortunately for me, two years before I had joined, an associated company had gone into liquidation. So, inherited and sitting on the shop floor virtually unused, were two relatively modern and up-to-date machines. Coincidentally, one was an English-built version of the Australian machinery my previous company had been trying to get me to agree to purchase. The other was German built. Thus the door was open, with a heaven-sent opportunity to evaluate both and compare them to existing equipment.

This was easily accomplished by fitting a range of established production tools into each machine in rotation. The results showed a positive improvement in output of 25% for the English machine, but up to 40% for the German equipment. Also product quality was more easily controlled, particularly so on the German machine.

The results were demonstrated to all interested parties, and even the previously dubious Works Manager seemed to be convinced. It was thus possible to make return on capital employed calculations in order to justify the replacement of obsolete equipment.

I invited the Sales Manager for the German machine supplier to quote for the supply of three machines. Hans (that really was his name) made a very competitive offer, which I was able to justify to the Board, so about three months later the modernisation of our equipment got off to a flying start.

The situation then settled down for some months. I had certainly upset a few people - I was not very popular in the accounts department for example - but the atmosphere at management meetings was now conducive to progress rather than confrontation.

The Production Manager left the company and I was promoted to the position. I was also appointed as Joint Trade Union Negotiator, with my signature being required on all agreement documents. How I achieved this position I was never sure; it was probably because no one else wanted the responsibility. This was perhaps understandable because at the time, in the motor industry generally, the trade unions seemed to be becoming very confrontational.

I soon discovered that this was no time to become complacent, for as a trade supplier you are subject to unsatisfactory events which are completely outside your control. We were due to commence production of a new set of components for a major customer. The procedure can vary, but in this case the product had been designed by the customer, including all the engineering and mould building details, together with quality control gauges. The tooling was part owned by the customer and part by us, the supplier, as was standard industry practice.

There were two production moulding tools, each with its own part number embossed onto the product. Both parts were to be identical, except one should have been a left hand version, the other right, but due to a mould design error they were both the same hand, except for the nine-digit part number identification.

The original test prototypes had been made correctly, but somehow the handing details had been misconfigured for the production tooling. We were thus unable to supply the correct sets of parts.

To say all hell broke loose would be a considerable understatement. The senior management from the customer descended on us at board room level, as their production line was stopped. I was called in to the meeting to find that the problem was being attributed to our failure to supply. I pointed out that the tooling design error by the customer's own engineering department, which had not been identified to their senior management, was the actual cause. What actually happened at their end I never found out, but suffice it to say that in those enlightened days people did not get golden handshakes for making major errors.

What was much more important was to solve the problem quickly. This was accomplished in less than three weeks by providing our own facility to remake the mould cavities. Our toolroom manager achieved this in an amazingly short time. I know he did much of the work himself, working through the night on a number of occasions. Splendid chap, Frank. He saved our collective bacon. Unfortunately he was also a worrier, and he suffered a fatal heart attack a few months later.

While all this was going on my sporting life had declined to nil. Obviously I was no longer playing cricket for my previous company. But during a meeting with the Trade Union representative, practice facilities for the works football team were discussed. I'm not sure how it came about, but the team needed a goalkeeper, and against my better judgement I must have volunteered, because I attended practice and was selected for the team. Fortunately my football boots had not accompanied my cricket gear into the dustbin as yet.

So my Saturday afternoon visits to watch Birmingham City were replaced once again by playing in the Birmingham Works League. Fortunately for everyone concerned, especially Barbara and Kim, this did not last long. Without regular practice, I was not fit enough to play on a regular basis and after losing 5-2 against Rover Solihull in a cup match in which at least two of the goals were my fault, I decided to retire before I suffered the embarrassment of being dropped. My boots were now definitely going in the bin. This was 1967, the year after England won the World Cup.

I thought at the time that this would definitely be the end of my involvement in competitive sport, but little did I know that some years later I would be taking part in an extremely demanding competitive alternative, together with Barbara. More about that later.

The complications and constant stress of all the above probably meant that I was neglecting my home life. I know I usually arrived home late in the evening after Kim had gone to bed and I quite often had a need to go off to sort out some problem or other.

My reading was almost exclusively confined to technical publications, trade magazines and journals. I must have been a real bore.

But I was always looking for the next step on the ladder, and I spotted it, or so I thought, through a widely-publicised job as Manager, Director Designate for a company based in New Milton on the south coast. The salary on offer was about double my existing earnings, and the company concerned produced its own range of proprietary products, an environment I was used to. Following application, I was invited for interview and Barbara and I travelled down to New Milton in Hampshire for the interview and to size up the area. I was short listed, apparently only one other candidate remaining on the list. We travelled down for a second interview, this time also looking at the available housing, local schools and general facilities.

A week later, I was disappointed to be thanked for my application but advised that the other candidate had been appointed. End of story, I thought, but no, five weeks later I received a letter to say that the appointment had not worked out. Would I still be interested in the position?

I should have been suspicious, but off we went again. The Viva was almost on autopilot by now. There was an additional incentive included in the package offered, in the form of a free company bungalow, and we were given the keys to inspect the property. On arrival we passed the man who I realised later must have been the previous appointee, because he said, 'Be very wary before accepting this job'. Just sour grapes, I thought. Anyway this bungalow just about sealed the deal, especially when it turned out to back onto a beautiful park area, with the local school in sight across the green.

The position seemed too good to turn down, despite the need for Kim to change school and moving away from close family. So all arrangements were made and I gave in my notice, which was not too well received, because I had a lot of uncompleted changes in midstream. Our house in Hollywood was put up for sale and we moved lock, stock and barrel down to Hampshire. Kim started in the new school and I began in the new job on the first day of the month.

Almost immediately things started to turn sour. On the first day after the Chairman had introduced me to the senior management, following an initial tour, he asked the Works Manager to give me a breakdown of the working schedules and various management structures. During the discussions he mentioned that he had a young daughter who was on dialysis and waiting for a kidney transplant. I expressed sympathy, but did not think much more about it.

Over the following few days I made myself familiar with the product range and manufacturing systems. At the end of the first week the Chairman invited me for a progress discussion, at the end of which, without warning, he said, 'I want you to dismiss the Works Manager and take over his function as part of your duties'.

I wrestled with this problem over the weekend. I now began to realise the significance of the warning given by the previous appointee. I concluded that it would not be right to take this course of action.

The following week I told the Chairman of my conclusion. He did not seem too concerned about this. The following day, however, he informed me that he no longer considered me suitable for the original senior management role and offered me a production management job at half the salary. The full significance of the warning given to me dawned. Obviously this was a repeat of the previous successful applicant's 'unsuitability'.

What a disaster. This much-reduced offer was completely unacceptable. I was shattered to have been conned and rejected in this way, but Barbara was very supportive, even though we had a traumatic upset in moving a long distance away from the family, together with the disturbance to Kim's schooling.

So the job search was on. We took advantage of the remaining month in the bungalow and arranged removal back to our Hollywood house, which fortunately was still unsold. I did not notice, but mistakenly included in our furniture for the return journey was a set of wooden stepladders, part of the bungalow equipment. These still remain in my garden shed and do occasionally get used 46 years later. They are certainly the only positive practical outcome of that disastrous episode.

I did actually consider a change into special purpose machinery sales, but after receiving an attractive job offer, I decided I did not want to become involved in constantly travelling away from home. I had continued to maintain contact with my first employer, and knowing that they had not succeeded in finding a satisfactory replacement for me during the intervening two years, I decided to enquire if they would be interested in my return.

Fortunately, I had applied at just the right time, for they were becoming increasingly concerned about a lack of progress in my specialist area. The Divisional Director, out of necessity, was attempting to perform the function alongside his other duties. I was thus welcomed back with unexpected enthusiasm, actually with higher status than I had previously enjoyed.

There is no doubt that there would be an opportunity to use the knowledge and extra experience I had gained from my time away to benefit both the company and my future progress. So ended my 'grass is greener' manoeuvres.

CHAPTER 9

PROGRESSION AND PROMOTION YEARS

————⟨❧⟩————

After that little adventure in Hampshire we had now moved back to our Hollywood house, only two miles from my place of employment, and Kim was back in her original school, having been away only about a month.

It was back to my old firm to pick up the threads, and many things became apparent during my first few weeks. Firstly, the systems I had designed and introduced to measure efficiency and productivity were fortunately still in place and being clerically maintained. Unfortunately, analysis of the results showed declining levels of productivity and high scrap rates, yet action to find and correct the faults and developing problems had not been taken.

Without going into technical details, this would involve me spending many weeks on the shop floor, optimising processing conditions together with, most importantly, re-establishing checking procedures. Because the personnel were mostly unchanged from the time when the systems had first been introduced, this was fairly easy to achieve, especially when productivity and consequent bonus earnings started to improve again.

On the practical manufacturing side, I was concerned to find that the equipment modernisation had continued in my absence, but I did not even begin to agree with the purchases made. For example, they had gone ahead and bought two of the Australian-built machines I had previously baulked at purchasing. They were showing some productivity improvements over the in-house equipment, but I knew for an absolute fact from my practical tests that they were by no means the best purchase.

Also the company, during my absence, had become involved in supplying a limited range of plastic components for the cosmetics industry, and to facilitate this they had purchased what was thought to be the best equipment to achieve this. The Canadian machine concerned, very aptly named 'Husky', was almost certainly the fastest machine in the world at the time, but it had been designed almost exclusively for producing very thin wall disposable items, and was completely unsuitable for all but one of the targeted cosmetic components.

How the justification to purchase this equipment had

been made was a mystery to me, for its potential capacity was being very poorly used, with no products on the marketing horizon to improve this. It was completely incompatible with the rest of the production range.

Very fortunately, a solution to this was to present itself. Metal Box of Swindon were the only other users of the Husky machine in the UK, for the production of aerosol can tops. When their capacity became overloaded, the machine supplier referred them to us for help. It was more than convenient to be able to offer our spare capacity for a very profitable return.

These events turned out to be of particular additional interest to me, because when the Metal Box Works Manager, John Taylor, visited to finalise the arrangements, he turned out to be the very man who had held the aborted New Milton job before my accidental meeting with him as he had left the bungalow a few years earlier, when he had warned me to be wary about taking the position. He had also apparently been offered the lower salaried job before leaving.

Anyway the company was very keen to continue with investment in new equipment. I was asked to attend a two-day seminar by the new UK manufacturer of the Australian-type machine, now to be built in Sheffield. With the benefit of my prior knowledge, having used almost identical equipment during my time at Wilmot Breeden, I was able to make an objective analysis of any proposed or current improvements in this equipment.

On my return, my convictions were unchanged, so the original impasse of a few years before was raising its head again. However I now had experience and facts on my side. How to get my message across was the problem.

I decided to produce a report which would include the technical specifications of all the comparable machines available. By now there were about ten different machine manufacturers making comparable machines. A points system gave an overall best buy conclusion. To my satisfaction, my preferred German machine came out top. The next move was to copy the result to all interested and some not-so-interested parties, including the Main Board members.

I was very pleased, about two weeks later, when I was asked to commence the updating of our production facilities by justifying the purchase of the first three new German machines, based on a return on capital employed of 20%. This was the start of a consistent capital expenditure programme, under my direction, extending over a period of 15 to 20 years.

Coinciding with all this hurly burly activity at work, we moved house from the modern estate, which Barbara had never really liked, to a 1930s rural house nearby, still in Hollywood but with open fields front and rear. Kim had been visiting the local riding school for lessons from the age of about five, but now there was a farm with stables and horses at the bottom of the garden.

Of course it was not long before she wanted her own pony. Now I knew absolutely nothing about horses, so we asked my sister Prudence, who had always been very much involved and had her own horse, if she would try out a pony we had selected as looking quite suitable for Kim. Just as well we did, because the pony turned out to be very unpredictable and actually threw her off.

Not to be deterred, another more suitable pony was sourced from a different seller. During the buying discussion, when I also arranged to purchase the saddle and other bits and pieces, I managed to display my ignorance by calling these items tackle instead of the correct term, tack. I saw the seller look at me with disdain, obviously thinking 'I've got a right idiot here'.

So began the daily trips to feed and ride the pony, which we called Candy. I was only very occasionally involved, as Barbara and Kim were the experts. My lack of gardening ability now extended to other rural activities.

I did become involved on one very significant occasion however. We had gone to check the pony's condition, and somehow she escaped through the gate into the lane. Off she trotted and I gave chase, running alongside - I must have thought I was Tom Mix (for the uninitiated, he was a cowboy from the silent movie era who jumped into the saddle from balconies or while running alongside his speeding nag). On second thoughts, in view of my stumbling progression, perhaps Hopalong Cassidy would have been closer to the mark - he was the one with the high-crowned white Stetson hat, from more modern talking westerns.

Anyway, regardless of all this, I could not get my Wellington-clad foot into the stirrup. Fortunately Candy came to a halt, not because of my pathetic endeavours, but I think out of embarrassment, as she did not want to be laughed at any more by the watching crowd.

I have never had the slightest desire to take to the saddle since that day. I decided I would stick to motor cars - at least they break down in a much more predictable way.

During this period Barbara and I resurrected our interest in ballroom dancing, firstly at a social level. We probably went dancing on a weekly basis, usually to the White Lion, Portway in Warwickshire, which was a very popular venue for Midland social dancers, mainly due to the excellent Phil Phillips Dance Band. We made many friends, particularly Phil himself and his wife Chris and also Ted, the guitarist in the band, and his wife Pearl. Phil, being a marvellous clarinettist and alto sax player, was always in great demand, both with his own band and individually for the remainder of the week, but Barbara and I did spend many happy Sunday afternoons together with Kim and Phil's children, Steve, Sue and Wendy. Not to forget our first Cairn Terrier,

Jason. Interestingly, Sue studied piano and violin under Phil's initial guidance and eventually became a violinist with the Birmingham Symphony Orchestra, travelling the world with them on tour.

I somehow became very involved in the Parent Teacher Association at Kim's school, and helped to organise the fund-raising activities, including the annual fête, cheese and wine evenings and social dances. Because most helpers were also involved in normal daytime jobs, all these activities seemed to progress in what could only be described as constant chaos.

For my part I eventually became treasurer, as no one else seemed to want the job. I recall at one annual fête that a raffle was organised, the top prize being a football signed by all the Aston Villa first team, with the ball to be presented by an international star player. This attracted a tremendous amount of interest and many ticket purchases. The only problem was that that idiot player (I will refrain from mentioning his name) forgot to bring the autographed ball.

Thankfully, when Kim left school to start working for a professional audit company, where she met the young man who she would eventually marry a few years later in 1979, I was able to extract myself from these duties, but I was given life membership of the association in recognition of my services.

In 1982 we became proud grandparents to our beautiful first granddaughter, Gemma Louise.

We were of course still involved with social ballroom dancing and decided to try out competition dancing at beginner level. We were hooked when we went to our first local competition, which inspired us to aim for the standard of the higher level competitors we saw on that day. Even though we had not had the essential input of proper coaching, we made the beginners' final.

So, what would eventually prove to be a very important sporting and career activity commenced. Most people, including us at the start, do not realise the intensity of training and the time and financial expenditure necessary to achieve even a modest degree of success. A fully-qualified professional coach for weekly private instruction, together with attendance at practice sessions, is very time and cash consuming, but essential for progress.

After progressing through from beginner grade to novice level, the need to have the correct specialist made ballroom tail suit and ladies' dance dress as well as Latin outfits, which are not allowed at beginner level but necessary in the higher grades, became an expensive requirement. After all, you don't wear your gardening clothes to play football or cricket. I remember my first tail suit cost £220.

Many couples were content to continue at novice level for years on end, just for the satisfaction of being involved. This was not for us however, as we were determined to progress through if possible to championship level.

Towards this end, very early on, we entered the UK Novice of the Year event. Disaster struck about twelve days prior to the competition, when I developed a very badly swollen and extremely painful right big toe. Now of course I already had my gammy left ankle to contend with, which I could usually control by keeping moving and avoiding sharp unplanned movements. This was different however. I thought at first I must have broken my toe, so I bound it tightly, but this made it worse. Now I had to learn the supreme skill of limping on two legs at the same time! I do now offer lessons in this, but they must be pre booked at an extortionate fee.

Anyway, a visit to the doctor was obviously called for. To my astonishment he diagnosed gout as the problem. After a few days taking the prescribed anti-inflammatory tablets the condition subsided considerably and we were actually able to compete on the day.

My movement was restricted somewhat, so although we had been the favourites to win, we only finished second. However we were more than satisfied with that. I think the judges were probably watching Barbara more than me, especially as we had a very good write up in the weekly Dance News, with worldwide distribution.

At this point we began to realise the intense level of

training and fitness levels required. At the start I was perhaps a little overweight at 13 stone 2lbs, but this dropped to 11 stone 3 lbs during the first year. It is an indisputable fact that to achieve even a modicum of success, ballroom dancing is far more physically demanding than football or cricket. A series of five dance heats would use every reserve of stamina.

Anyway, this was the start of our progression through the novice, intermediate, pre championship and eventually championship grades over a period of many years. To achieve this target did involve a considerable amount of travelling. Most competitions were on Sundays, and we would perhaps go up to Leeds one week, then the following week it would be Bristol or London. Usually we would arrive at the event in the early afternoon and very often not leave until after midnight, perhaps not arriving home until 2.30 am, having then to get up at seven in the morning for work.

During this period, we actually had to concentrate more exclusively on the Latin American discipline due to time constraints. Having won nine pre-championship trophies we moved exclusively into the championship grade. We knew that we were hardly likely to reach the very top - age was against us, as we had started too late and were probably fifteen years older than most of the opposition, who also probably had twenty years more experience, having started competing as young children.

We usually managed to reach the final of the senior regional championships and actually won the Worcestershire, South West of England and South Wales events, being ranked thirteenth in the UK. We reached the semi-final of the British championship at the Winter Gardens in Blackpool before retiring from competition, due to work pressures alongside our new retail business venture.

During this period we had various holidays, including a visit to Jersey. Unfortunately the flight was on a very old and bumpy Dakota aircraft, which succeeded in putting Barbara off flying completely.

Meanwhile, whilst all this social activity was going on, my work was becoming increasingly time-consuming. My first two-day trip abroad for the company, for the express purpose of showing an associate company's technicians in Holland the details of a specific manufacturing process, was very successful and proved to be important in securing my future.

Having succeeded in overcoming the problems which had developed in my department during the two years I was away and instigating the equipment replacement programme, I was promoted to Production Manager for the Division. This I realised was not too popular a development among my peers, so one of my first problems was to overcome this, shall we say, resentment. I did this by being helpful almost to the extreme in all areas, while at the same time watching my back. This was probably the most stressful two years in my management career, but eventually things settled down.

We had very close ties with two major US companies, producing very similar ranges but on a much larger scale, and historically many parts of the product ranges had been jointly developed. Thus I made my first visit to America in 1973, initially visiting Goody Products in New York City. I recall that I was booked with a colleague, Don Hogarth from our Australian factory, into the Pennsylvania Hotel of Glenn Miller fame - Pennsylvania 6-5000 was still the telephone number.

We stayed only one night, as it seemed to have become rather seedy relative to its imagined previous status. Don ordered a boiled egg for breakfast and it came almost completely uncooked. When he complained, the waiter said the egg boiling machine must have gone wrong. We struggled to understand what an egg boiling machine could possibly be other than a pan of boiling water. Perhaps it was because we both came from very backward countries.

While Don flew down to Birmingham Alabama to visit the main Goody manufacturing facility, I visited Foster Grant, the sunglass manufacturers in Worcester, New York State. The production facilities were very automated even in those early days, and I found the principles of this of considerable interest. Every sunglass lens used, for example, was automatically impact tested.

I then travelled down to join Don in Alabama on the following day. Production at Goody's was massive in scale, probably by a factor of ten compared to both the UK and Australian factories, so the product development and tooling costs for new products were obviously much easier to justify. Against this, when compared with Foster Grant, the main production equipment seemed old and there was very little automation.

Don then departed for Australia, but I arranged to fly back up to Boston, in order to visit a company developing central production control systems before travelling back to England.

I was promoted to Director for the Plastics Division shortly afterwards. I was then able to ensure that progress was accelerated in the automation of the component production and packaging methods. For example, in conjunction with the now almost completely updated range of processing machinery, we introduced a system of automated material delivery from central silo storage and colouring at the machine, using unique in-house designed and purpose-built equipment. This gave us considerable flexibility, as well as a commercial advantage, in satisfying our customers' requirements.

Product packaging was gradually changing to flow line systems to reflect the modern need for secure blister product presentation.

My specialist area still required a considerable proportion of my time during the following years, but I did ensure progress in more general disciplines. For example, computer stock control was to be introduced to replace the existing clerically-intensive system, which had proved to be very unreliable. It was essential as sales volumes accumulated that a logical component part numbering system was developed so that available free stock was known. An essential feature of this had to be component numbers, which would not be difficult to relate to specific parts on the shop floor.

In this respect, because of my previous experience, I was adamant that this could not be just a sequence of numbers, as was the company accounts department's target, because it would be easier for the typist to enter. It also needed to incorporate alpha characters, providing an abbreviated description in order to avoid incorrect identification of components on the shop floor and in the various warehouses.

My proposed principle was accepted, I think grudgingly. In order to ensure that this was done logically I undertook to develop the part identification system myself. Using the principle of an existing divisional identification number and a usually pre-existing part number, followed by the devised three-character description, I took each of the division's end sales products onto my desk and plodded through the process, entering the results onto matrix sheets for clerical entry to the computer. Because there were hundreds of sales items, the whole process took about six months to give a comprehensive and accurate free component stock report on a weekly basis, but it was extremely satisfying to be able to plan production using much more accurate and up-to-date information. This of course had the net effect of reducing ongoing clerical requirements.

There were of course considerable other benefits. The stock could be valued, for example, on a continuous basis, on the computer, making the monthly accounts more accurate than using historical gross profit percentages, as was the previous method.

In conjunction with this, the accuracy of initial stocktaking was of paramount importance. Having discovered some very unsatisfactory historical inaccuracies, which had impacted on the success of the computer stock control, I established that most of the problems had been generated through a lack of standard counting and calculating procedures.

Having discussed this problem with the Chief Accountant, I proposed the introduction of a standard card based counting system, whereby all accumulated totals could be double checked later. Equally important, the official auditors would be able to make satisfactory test counts.

This principle was introduced for the whole company. As I was the prime mover in this project, when the auditors arrived for the annual stock check, I was given the responsibility to explain the principles and kick start the new procedures.

Whilst all this was going on, developments on the more practical side were continuing apace. We were constantly exploring improving technologies, which involved many visits to trade shows both in England and Germany. Our ever-improving production facilities were now starting to include robotics and computer process control to an increasing degree. In addition packaging methods were becoming more automated and streamlined, and many decorating and assembly techniques were being developed.

During this time we had various visits to our production facilities from our associate company in the USA. They were very impressed with our in-house developed production systems, particularly our unique material colouring at the machine system, which they decided to adopt for their much larger scale manufacturing units, so they were provided with all the engineering details.

In 1987 I made my second visit to the USA, including this in a solo fact-finding round-the-world journey, visiting New York, Atlanta, Columbus and Birmingham Alabama, Los Angeles, Hawaii, Sydney and Melbourne Australia, Hong Kong and Taiwan, all in a period of nineteen days.

Although my previous visit to the USA in 1973 had gone without any travelling and accommodation hitches, this time, due to a complete change in administration personnel, involving a new company secretary and accountant, there would prove to be many errors for me to resolve throughout the journey. All the difficulties were in fact caused by appointing a new but obviously incompetent travel agent to plan the details.

The first problem arose when I arrived in Columbus. I had been issued with Thomas Cook travellers' cheques, but these were not recognised, nor apparently at the time were they acceptable in the deep south. I had to rely on the host company to settle my pre-booked hotel and ancillary costs. An appointment with their company bankers had to be made in order to cash the offending travellers' cheques prior to my onward journey.

The second problem arose on my arrival in Los Angeles, when I found that the hotel booked for me was actually about three thousand miles away in downtown New York! I managed to make alternative short notice accommodation arrangements, but these proved to be not very salubrious. The bed sheets actually had holes in them at foot level, in which my toes kept getting caught. One uncomfortable night there was more than enough.

The third difficulty came during my stay in Hawaii. As my flight was due to arrive in the evening, I had specifically requested that two nights' accommodation should be booked, in order that over the weekend I would be able to visit Pearl Harbour and other areas of interest.

Sure enough a good job had been done here, two nights had been booked and I was able to see the sights. One serious problem, however - the travel agent had failed to allow for the International Date Line, so when I arrived at the airport to continue my onward journey to Australia, I was told I was a day too late and had missed my flight. This had apparently caused great consternation in Australia, as they had arranged a welcoming barbecue in my honour, but as they put it, 'We have lost a Brit' - panic stations. Anyway all was eventually well, as I was able to book onto the next flight. The airline were quite used to this type of occurrence.

Apart from these avoidable travel problems, It was very satisfying during my visits to Columbus and Birmingham Alabama to see that our American associate company had adopted, on a massive scale, compared to our relatively small facilities, my principle of material colouring at the machine, the design and engineering details of which I had provided during their visit to our plant in England only two years before.

During my visit to our Australian subsidiary, I was

able to explore and draw a final conclusion to the long-standing saga of the virtues and viability of purchasing the Australian-built injection moulding machine, as described in chapter 8.

They had long since concluded that other equipment was much more productive and were now using machines built in Taiwan. I was able to do some production studies in Sydney, which very clearly established that my now very much updated German-built equipment back home in England was 30% more productive. I did however take the opportunity to visit the machine builder in Taiwan, to find that the engineering standards were not conducive to produce equipment which would be expected to withstand the required 24/7 use for an extended lifespan.

Shortly after my return I was given additional responsibility for a second manufacturing site and appointed Manufacturing Director.

CHAPTER 10

THE FASHION BUSINESS

At this time there was a major development on the home front which would prove to be very important for our future prosperity. Barbara had always been very keen on fashion, and the opportunity came up to purchase a ladies' fashion boutique. It was too good a chance to resist, so we took the plunge, moving from our Hollywood home to live on the shop premises in Studley. We had to do considerable research before committing to the purchase, and of course we needed to present a viable business plan to the bank before the project could be started. The target was to take the existing business more upmarket, renaming the shop 'Posh Frocks'.

Our second granddaughter, Kirsty, had arrived in 1986, and the Posh Frocks retail business started up in 1988. Thanks to Barbara's eye for fashion and selection of stock, the target was more than achieved. Turnover was 50% higher than the previous business and well above the original business plan, with net profit in excess of 20%.

About once every other month, usually on a Monday, I would take a day of my annual holiday entitlement from my day job and we would go to various London wholesalers for replacement stock. I was just assistant labourer and driver to the experts, Barbara and Kim. With Kim helping to run the shop, both granddaughters, Gemma and Kirsty, were frequently with us after school, and very often stayed overnight.

Because the shop and later our Dancintime business did not leave us much free time for holidays, we had a static caravan which we kept about one hour's drive away, and we visited it as often as duty would allow. On many occasions Gemma and Kirsty would come with us, especially on school half terms. A very happy time was had by all, including our second Cairn Terrier, Louis.

In 1992 we were invited to join Kim and Dennis, Gemma and Kirsty on holiday in Mallorca, so we decided to take the opportunity and close the shop for a week to join them. We had a very enjoyable time together, even if Barbara did have to force herself to endure the flights.

The only other time we closed the shop was to run a stall at the combined Motor Show and Ideal Home Exhibition at the National Exhibition Centre. We did all the organising, including the stand building ourselves, rather than sub contract to specialists. This was a very stressful and time-consuming operation, but very rewarding in the end, for we did gain important publicity in a Birmingham Mail editorial. Our presence was mentioned alongside a number of high-profile national organisations. Even more importantly, our stock sold very well, because while a male visitor would have his attention riveted to the latest new car, his wife or girlfriend wandered off to the Ideal Home stands, to come unexpectedly across the Posh Frocks display. Out of sight and out of mind, they had a ball. My duties were of course not selling; I was just there for security, to move things about and to help with transactions. Mind you, at the height of the pressure I did actually sell a pair of Gina designer shoes for £230.

Credit card transactions then required a confirmation telephone call to the card issuer for an authorisation code reference number. In order to accomplish this we had one of the early Motorola so-called mobile phones, although it was actually larger and heavier than a house brick. In the interests of security I had chained it to the stand structure. This was just as well, as all the stands adjacent to us where the staff had more modern and smaller mobiles had them stolen. We thus had an influx of stand holders adding to our pressures by asking for help and of course getting it, to facilitate their transaction confirmations.

At work it was becoming increasingly obvious, under the guidance of a new younger generation of owning family company main board directors, that the organisation was changing direction towards a more marketing-inspired business rather than one which was manufacturing orientated. This manifested itself in a desire for ready-made goods from the Far East, rather than developing in-house products. This was but a microcosm of what was happening in British manufacturing industries generally at the time, primarily driven by very low labour costs in the supplying countries in the Far East. Against this background it became increasingly difficult to justify new projects.

In my capacity as Manufacturing Director I was involved in many discussions on new range developments. In particular at the time it was very much in vogue to be associated with high-profile personality names, for example the men's jewellery range targeted Seve Ballesteros and Noel Edmonds, although both ranges were abject failures. However we had reasonable success on the hair ornamentation side following product meetings with Mary Quant, who proved to be knowledgeable on development criteria, including time scales, as well as having of course a great aptitude for style.

Mary also seemed very impressed with our unique

ability to match moulded component colours within a 24-hour time cycle, a facility developed by myself and not available from our competitors. At our second meeting she presented me with a signed copy of her book Colours by Quant.

Unfortunately her assistant was not at all compliant on the current undeniably long product development time lag. She was in fact, determined to press ahead with short time scale purchases of existing items from the Far East for branding to our Mary Quant range.

As our own marketing department was already being drawn down this avenue and could not be persuaded of the eventual futility of this course of action, where other competitive importers could undercut and eventually destroy profit margins, the die was cast. The result, very little home manufactured product was included in the Mary Quant range, and it was successful for the short period I predicted. I was able to turn this situation to my own advantage by purchasing some of the drastically written-down stock for our Posh Frocks business.

The answer to these new product development challenges could and should have been the adoption of computer-aided design and development, where a stereographic modelling system, the forerunner to 3D printing, was available, to be allied to our state-of-the-art, low labour content, automated manufacturing processes.

In fact a new product development system, targeted specifically at our main manufacturing area, had been developed by Delcam at the Aston Science Park in Birmingham. I arranged a demonstration seminar for all senior executives in order to show the way forward.

Following the presentation and my proposal to adopt this course of action, I was advised that manufacturing capital expenditure was to be restricted to projects predicted to return 40% per annum return on capital employed, rather than the 20% previously used. Thus the company's direction away from a manufacturing future was reinforced. The fact that 95 of the new computer-aided design systems from Delcam were now operational, 92 of them in Taiwan and Hong Kong, was not considered relevant.

The lack of any new product development resulted in the closing down of the toolroom in which I had served my apprenticeship many years before. The writing was now really on the wall for any possible resurrection of a viable future for the company. The newly employed Financial Director and Chief Accountant seemed an unstoppable force. Much of the company's manufacturing expertise and equipment acquired during the previous very successful 125-year history was sold, in many cases to our Far East competitors. This situation was even compounded by sending our engineers and technicians out to China to instruct employees there on how they should be used. I made it quite clear that I profoundly disagreed with these actions. The result of all this was a declining sales revenue. The marketing targets for our now mostly imported product range were not being attained, and the company contracted down to one site only, with many redundancies.

It was not too much of a surprise then that in 1991, following a total of forty years employment, I was called into the Chairman's office to be given a letter to read offering me the choice of a redundancy package or early retirement. Although I was unaware of this until after my meeting, both the Managing Director and Engineering Director were also made redundant, but they were not near retirement age, so this was obviously a more significant blow for them.

Needless to say, as I had other irons in the fire, the early retirement option, even though I was only 58 years of age, seemed to be the most suitable in my circumstances. That decision was confirmed following a consultation with my accountant.

I did have a rather perverse sense of satisfaction some time afterwards when the company was the subject of a management buyout, involving, of course, the aforementioned Financial Director, and then within three years it became insolvent, ceased trading and was closed down. This must have been disappointing for the previous family owners to observe, when they had built the organisation up over a period of a hundred and thirty-five years.

All this was of little concern to Barbara and me, as I had a secure inflation-proofed pension and the fashion outlet was doing well. We decided to take advantage of our competitive dance experience by studying for a professional qualification with the International Dance Teachers' Association. We duly qualified, following a very intensive period of study, and started our own dance school business, 'Dancintime', early in 1993.

CHAPTER 11

THE DANCINTIME YEARS

Initially we operated the shop and the dance company together, but in 1995 we decided to concentrate our efforts entirely on the dance activities and close the retail outlet. We now had a large spare room which we converted into a dance studio, for use in addition to the local church and village halls. We also ran classes at Bromsgrove New College and two Sunday night ballroom and Latin classes at a further venue. We were generally very busy, especially so with private lessons.

The vogue for western line dancing had now become prominent, and although we found this fairly boring we had to go with the flow. I recall that in the end we were teaching 35 different dances, but no one could remember what we had taught a few weeks previously and there were new versions being choreographed almost on a daily basis. Nevertheless we had a demonstration team, the Studley Stompers, for local charity events. We were not unhappy when the demand for this activity reduced significantly.

In addition to ballroom and Latin instruction classes, we ran a weekly dance practice, social events, summer balls and Christmas party dances. Life was becoming perhaps a little too chaotic.

I recall for example, that we organised a ball to celebrate the Queen's Golden Jubilee and found we needed some extra party supplies during the afternoon of the big day. So off we dashed in the car, but I failed to notice that a new set of 40 mph speed cameras had been installed along our regular route. I suppose I was distracted by the purpose of the journey. This meant I managed to acquire speeding tickets for travelling at a modest 48 mph in both directions, along a very straight clear section of main road, thus gaining six points on my driving licence in one day, not to mention the accompanying fine, which effectively eradicated any profit we might have expected to make from that evening's function. Nevertheless the occasion went very well and an enjoyable time was had by all.

This level of activity continued for 14 years, during which time the BBC began its 'Strictly Come Dancing' series, which had a very positive effect on demand for our classes. To illustrate this we would normally have about 40 new members for a beginner class, but on one occasion in particular we had 115 people arrive to register. At the end of this period, demand for private lessons was at an all-time high. We were finding it extremely difficult, both now being in our seventies, to keep up with the continual pressures on our time, and after we had both succumbed to bouts of flu we decided to give up the classes and concentrate on private lessons. We restricted this activity to four nights per week and thus had the weekend, Saturday, Sunday (and Monday usually, but not always), free for the first time in over 14 years.

Unfortunately a few years later, Barbara needed a hip replacement, which did curtail our dance teaching activities for a short period. We continued teaching for a number of years until I became an octogenarian, but as demonstrating double reverse spins and ronda chasses with any degree of style does become difficult as you get more ancient, we finally decided to retire.

On reflection we were able to look back on 21 years of enjoyable teaching, for we had in that time taught upwards of 1500 people to dance, some to a very high standard.

Also of course, we met many interesting pupils. Almost invariably they would be professional people, for example, schoolteachers, members of the police force, doctors or business managers.

One couple, not long after we started teaching, were both gynaecologists. She was heavily pregnant, but they carried on with their lessons until about a week before the birth. I must admit that we were a little worried that she might trip or fall during class, but they could not have been better qualified to judge this for themselves and everything ended successfully.

Another couple were both police detective inspectors, and the husband was at the time interviewed on the television news in relation to a murder investigation he was leading.

Among the many other high-profile students, to name but a few, were an ex-Police Chief Constable, the Chief Investigator for the Law Society, the Chief Executive of a Local Authority, a retired Church of England vicar, a headmaster, many schoolteachers, including two Heads of Music, a professional ballet teacher, a Top Gear cameraman, a BBC production assistant, A married couple who were both British Airways Flight Commanders and two Inland Revenue Tax Inspectors. There were also a number of farmers, who, surprisingly to me, were very keen dancers. One of them was a chicken farmer who came for private lessons four or five times a week over a two-year period. Another farmer, a very experienced dancer, came to improve his skills. We also did the choreography for the local high school production of Grease.

We made many friends during our dancing years, in particular Barrington and Terry Mayne, who were very loyal and were still coming for sessions when we took the regrettable decision to retire.

As they say, all good things must come to an end, but this final combined episode of our varied and colourful careers was undoubtedly the most satisfying and enjoyable.

And of course we were very thrilled and proud when our granddaughter Kirsty presented us with our first great-grandson, Oliver Jack, in 2010.

CHAPTER 12

LOOKING BACK

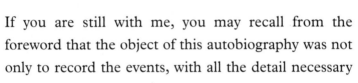

If you are still with me, you may recall from the foreword that the object of this autobiography was not only to record the events, with all the detail necessary to explain how progress was made, but to answer the implied questions 'Is it a disaster to fail the eleven plus'? and 'Is it a disaster not to go to university?'

My experiences are of course related to a failure to pass the eleven plus and thus qualify for a grammar school education, which had similar implications in 1944, as with the current time failure expectations at eighteen, regarding a university place.

So how did it go? I would argue reasonably well. My progression through from indentured apprenticeship to Manufacturing Director over a 43-year period, followed by a successful retail fashion business run with Barbara and Kim, which was then succeeded by 21 years running Dancintime, has brought me a relatively secure retirement.

Mind you, Gordon Brown and the Labour Government did not help. They almost completely destroyed the Final Salary Pension expectations of millions of deferred pensioners, by virtue of changes to the Corporation Tax regulations. They also tried very hard while they were in office to destroy the value of my private pension by allowing interpretation in 2006 of the 1997 Pension Protection Act, so that annual indexing for pensions earnings before 1997 were not protected. The Final Pensions Ombudsman's Ruling, supporting this interpretation, I refused to accept, for it went against all the promises made to me by the Trustees and the insurance company on my retirement in 1991.

Despite legal advice to the Trustees supporting the Ombudsman's conclusion, I persisted in my claim, writing possibly twenty letters and making countless telephone calls. The result was very satisfactory. Common sense finally reigned and indexing was to a large extent restored and corrected for the intervening seven years. Thus the basis of the original claim to the Ombudsman was satisfied, but at the expense of an extremely traumatic time.

Most importantly, Barbara survived all the turmoil I managed to create. We celebrated our Golden Wedding anniversary with a family party at Studley Castle in 2005, and we are still together after over 60 years. What a lucky chap I was at that Friday night fairground meeting back in 1951! She has supported me all that time through thick and thin.

We are happy that our immediate family, our daughter Kim and her husband Dennis, granddaughters Gemma and Kirsty and great-grandson Oliver live close by and visit frequently. My sister Prudence and Barbara's brother Martin also live fairly close. The only exception is my brother Tony, who lives in Australia - more about him later.

We are proud and pleased that the study and hard work gene has been passed down through the generations. Gemma has an Honours Degree in Business Studies, with subsequent postgraduate qualifications, and she is the most qualified person in her company. Kirsty is a fully qualified fitness trainer and dietitian.

Our residence, Terpsichore Cottage, which was originally built in 1743, has now been freed of all its commercial activities and been converted back into a spacious character home. We have come to a time when hopefully I have concluded my ridiculous car changing extravagances, for we have a very nice BMW coupé to potter about in. Mind you, I needed a cataract operation in order to continue driving. My vision is now probably better than it has been for possibly 20 years, which is amazing considering how quick and painless the procedure was.

This has had both positive and negative consequences. On the positive side, for example, the very complex professional Bluetooth radio in the BMW developed a fault. As it was out of guarantee, BMW stated that repairs were not possible, and the only option was replacement at £658. I baulked at this and contacted various independent auto radio experts, none of whom could offer a repair option. Although I have virtually no electronic or radio knowledge, I researched the problem and effected a repair to the unit for a total cost of £138. I would not have been able to do this without my vision improvement - and a considerable amount of determination.

On the negative side, my now laser-like vision has revealed that the previous few years' DIY efforts lack quality. I can see glaring faults all over the place. The problem is that I find it virtually impossible to get down on my hands and knees even to do simple jobs like painting skirting boards. I find it even more difficult to get back up. Mind you they do say the floor gets further away as you get older, but I sure wish there was a simple cataract-style procedure to correct this.

One positive piece of news is that my gammy left ankle, having given me trouble for 70 years, now seems, for some unaccountable reason, to be much improved. I look forward to a similar regeneration for some of my other wonky bits, though without too much faith.

Anyway to return to the analysis. By comparison with myself, my brother Tony passed the eleven-plus examination and benefited from a grammar school education. As we come from the same family background, we must presume he is more intelligent than me, but in the spirit of sibling rivalry I am not convinced, despite the fact that he later became a member of Mensa. Certainly he had one big advantage as a school leaver - following his education he had no trace of a Birmingham accent, just as our father had no trace of his Cockney background. Regardless of so-called conventional wisdom, this would undoubtedly give him important advantages later in life.

Tony then went on to employment at the Radar Research Establishment in Malvern, then into the army, where he studied electronics and obtained Higher National Certificate Qualification. On leaving the armed forces he joined EMI and progressed in the Television Broadcasting System Division. Although I am far from sure of the detail, eventually EMI were contracted for the installation of the Malaysian television broadcasting system and Tony was responsible for the planning and management of the installation, moving to Kuala Lumpur in order to accomplish the task. At the conclusion of the contract he was asked to stay on in the Far East and appointed Managing Director of EMI Malaysia.

He apparently sustained a very high life, commensurate with his position. Household servants were apparently part of the deal and he travelled extensively on business, to China and Japan for example. EMI were of course in the media and music fields at the time.

Tony's daughter Lisa became involved in equestrian show jumping to very high standard and Tony himself became very keen on polo, acquiring a string of ponies and meeting the Queen on her state visit. Presumable they discussed their joint interest in all things horsey.

But all good things eventually come to an end. EMI changed course and moved out of the media field and Tony was made responsible for selling the first medical body scanners in the South American region, which entailed being relocated to Argentina. He apparently did very well in this function, which involved marketing units which were each valued at £250,000. Of course he was also in the top world polo centre, and he took considerable advantage of this to develop his interests.

He returned to England to start his own business, having identified a gap in the polo mallet market, and manufactured mallets with glass fibre shafts. He secured a major market share, the Sultan of Brunei being among his customers. It must have been a considerable advantage to be in the polo playing set, with his string of ponies.

Eventually of course polo was replaced with the more sedentary sport of golf, and eventually he sold his manufacturing business and retired with his wife Frances to Australia, in order to be near their daughter Lisa and her husband Dominique, who had established a commercial photography business.

So the relevance of my own experiences can be put into context by comparison with Tony, who has been very successful, but in a different direction. So did success or failure at eleven plus make a difference? I leave it to the reader to judge.

ND - #0446 - 270225 - C10 - 203/127/11 - PB - 9781861512239 - Matt Lamination